Accelerated learning in the
Literacy Hour

Year 5

Sue Garnett

Published by Hopscotch Educational Publishing Ltd,
29 Waterloo Place, Leamington Spa CV32 5LA
(Tel: 01926 744227)

© 2002 Hopscotch Educational Publishing

Written by Susan Garnett
Series design by Blade Communications
Illustrated by Martha Hardy
Cover illustration by Debbie Clark
Printed by Clintplan, Southam

ISBN 1-904307-14-0

ACCELERATED LEARNING IN THE LITERACY HOUR

This series of books and the activity ideas are a direct result of the research into brain-based learning and multiple intelligences, how the brain works and how children learn. Howard Gardner sets out the results of this research in his books *Accelerated Learning in the Classroom* and *Accelerated Learning in Practice* (published by Network Educational Press Ltd). Information from his research and these books is given below.

Visual, Auditory and Kinaesthetic Learning (VAK)

People learn using their senses: their sense of hearing, sight and touch.

- 29% of us prefer to learn by seeing.
- 34% of us prefer to learn by hearing and using sound.
- 37% of us prefer to learn by doing.

It is important to know which is our preference, but it is just as important to learn to use the other senses too.

If we are to maximise children's learning, we should be aware of the children's strengths and not only provide them with activities that they prefer, but also give them access to all three types of learning so that they will learn new skills.

We remember:
- 20% of what we see
- 30% of what we hear
- 40% of what we say
- 50% of what we do
- 90% of what we see, hear, say and do.

Therefore, it is vital that you deliver lessons in such a way that there is variety, i.e. by using visual, auditory and kinaesthetic activities. You should provide input that covers all three types of learning. This may be done during the course of a lesson or over a series of lessons.

It is important that you provide a balanced curriculum covering the three types of learning just as you would provide a balanced diet.

Multiple Intelligences (MI)

Howard Gardner identified the Seven Plus One Intelligences (this has now become the Nine Intelligences). He said that people have different types of intelligences and that they are better at some than others. All the Nine Intelligences are important. All children are intelligent in some way.

The Nine Intelligences are:
- logical (Number/order smart)
- linguistic (Word smart)
- visual/spatial (Picture smart)
- interpersonal (People smart)
- intrapersonal (Myself smart)
- physical (Body smart)
- naturalistic (Naturalistic smart)
- musical (Music smart)
- spiritual.

Children benefit from a balance of activities which can enhance their preferred learning style. But it is also important to introduce them to other types of learning to strengthen and develop those with which they are not as confident. Providing a range and balance of activities will maximise their learning.

A balanced approach to learning

Visual, auditory and kinaesthetic learning fit in really well with the Nine Intelligences.

Example
Lesson objective – individually, to produce a leaflet to save the school.
The children would be learning visually.
The children would also be using several of the Nine Intelligences, i.e. linguistic, visual/spatial, intrapersonal and logical.

What is this book?

This book is a teacher resource. It provides a series of ideas to use in the classroom that will develop and maximise children's learning.

It provides visual, auditory and kinaesthetic activities to achieve the text level objectives of the National Literacy Strategy.

It also includes references to the Nine Intelligences.

This book will help towards enabling ALL children to be successful. It helps you to reach all of the children more of the time.

How does this book work?

Each lesson plan contains a literacy objective (text level), a whole class starter activity, ideas for group work (visual, auditory and kinaesthetic activities) and a plenary session. Each lesson also contains three sheets:

Sheet 1
This is a model that you share with the children.

Sheet 2
This sheet gives information on the three activities (visual, auditory and kinaesthetic) that you can use with the children to achieve the objective. You could split the children into groups according to their preferred learning style, or cover all the activities over a period of time. Children with special educational needs could cover the style they are most likely to be successful with.

Sheet 3
This is the children's worksheet. They may use it to make notes or plan their work.

If there are adult helpers in the class, they can work with a group of children on one of the objectives.

Recognising children's preferred learning styles

Below are lists of activities that the different types of learner enjoy doing. Over a period of time, teachers should try to ensure that children receive a balance from each list.

VISUAL LEARNERS

They learn best through seeing.

How can you recognise a visual learner?
They speak with their hands. They like to point things out. They speak rapidly.

What do they enjoy?
- Writing
- Drawing
- Computers
- OHPs
- Television
- Posters
- News reports
- Books
- Diaries
- Letters
- Key words
- Wall displays
- Films/videos
- Interactive whiteboards
- Interactive displays
- Arrow charts
- Flow charts
- Graphs
- Diagrams
- Pictures
- Mind maps

AUDITORY LEARNERS

They learn best through sound.

How can you recognise an auditory learner?
They like to hum, sing or whistle while doing activities.
They like to give and receive instructions verbally.

What do they enjoy?
- Audio tapes/CDs
- Radio programmes
- Circle time
- Hot seating
- Lectures
- Show and tell
- Debates/discussion
- School council
- Point of view
- Music and sound effects
- Interviews/interviewing
- Reporting
- Dance
- Drama

KINAESTHETIC LEARNERS

They learn best through movement.

How can you recognise a kinaesthetic learner?
They like to move about the classroom and touch things.
They get restless sitting down. They like physical activities.
They like to demonstrate or model. They fidget.

What do they enjoy?
- Role play and dressing up
- Show and tell
- Making things
- Modelling and collage
- Murals
- Puppet and mask making
- Flap books and concertina books
- Outdoor lessons
- Field trips
- Outdoor pursuits
- PE

- Dance
- Gym
- Music and Movement
- Brain gym
- Performances

How to find out what type of learner a child is

On page 6 there is a questionnaire. The children can either be given this to complete themselves or be helped by an adult to complete it.

The key to the questionnaire is given on page 7. For example, if the answer given to the first question by a child is 'Yes' then that indicates 'kinaesthetic'.

The results may show that the child has a dominant learning style or they may show that he or she has several learning styles.

The idea is to provide you, the teacher, with valuable information about the children so that you are better able to help them with their learning.

What kind of learner am I?

Name _____   Class _____

1. I like making things.	Yes	No
2. I like watching films.	Yes	No
3. I like listening to music.	Yes	No
4. I like listening to story tapes.	Yes	No
5. I like designing posters.	Yes	No
6. I like acting.	Yes	No
7. I like sport and playing out.	Yes	No
8. I like drawing.	Yes	No
9. I like lessons outdoors.	Yes	No
10. I like school trips.	Yes	No
11. I like dancing.	Yes	No
12. I like writing.	Yes	No
13. I like talking.	Yes	No
14. I like show and tell.	Yes	No
15. I like speaking in front of others.	Yes	No
16. I like debating and discussing.	Yes	No
17. I like drawing diagrams.	Yes	No
18. I like looking at the blackboard.	Yes	No
19. I like using whiteboards.	Yes	No
20. I like to talk while I work.	Yes	No
21. I like moving about.	Yes	No
22. I like reading.	Yes	No

What kind of learner am I? (Answer key)

1. K
2. V
3. A
4. A
5. V
6. K
7. K
8. V
9. K
10. K
11. K
12. V
13. A
14. A
15. A
16. A
17. V
18. V
19. V
20. A
21. K
22. V

Count up how many of each type they have.

> **Example**
> Jack Barnes   Class 5
>
> Visual = 0
> Auditory = 3
> Kinaesthetic = 6
>
> Dominant learning style = kinaesthetic

If a child circles all the yes answers, then they have no preferred learning style.

If they circle yes to 1, 6, 7, 9, 10, 11, 21 then they are a kinaesthetic learner.

If they circle yes to 2, 5, 8, 12, 17, 18, 19, 22 then they are a visual learner.

If they circle yes to 3, 4, 13, 14, 15, 16, 20 then they are an auditory learner.

Most children have a dominant learning style. If you give them the appropriate type of learning activity, then they will learn. For example, give a kinaesthetic learner things to make and things to do.

It is also important to give children a variety of activities, not just those from their own preferred learning style, in order that they develop new skills.

Children can be told what kind of learner they are. If they understand how they learn best, they can help themselves.

Writing in the same style as another writer

Literacy objective

- To write new characters into a story in the manner of the writer.

What you need

- Modelling clay and tools
- A tape recorder/Dictaphone
- Photocopies of pages 10 and 12
- Felt-tipped pens

Whole class starter

- Give each child a copy of the 'Bog Creature' sheet on page 10 or display it on an OHP or interactive whiteboard.

- Tell the children that they are going to work on characters. Read the story with them. Tell them that this is the opening to a story.

- Ask the children the following questions.

  - This is the opening to a story. How do we know it is the opening?

  - Why is a story opening important?

  - What kind of story is this – for example, mystery, fairytale, science fiction? How do you know? What is the story about?

  - How does the writer begin this story?

  - What is the setting for the story?

  - Who is the main character?

- Now look at the words the author has chosen to describe the character – 'slimy', 'bulbous eyes' and 'moved slowly'. With the children, think of other words to describe this creature. Use a thesaurus to help you.

- Look at how the author uses the conditional tenses – 'would' and 'could' – in the story. Ask the children to find the words and highlight or underline them. This is the author's style. Why do the children think she does this?

- The writer uses descriptive language to make the scene visual. She uses adjectives, similes and alliteration. Challenge the children to find all the examples of these and to highlight them. Say that if they were to extend the story in the same style, they would have to use the conditional tense and descriptive language.

- What do they think happens next in the story?

- Tell the children that they are now going to create a new character for the story in the style of the writer and then finish the story in their own way, whether written, verbally or illustratively.

Independent/group work

From the activities on page 11, either:

- select the most appropriate activity for each child/group according to whether they are kinaesthetic, auditory or visual learners and organise three separate working groups

or

- begin with the kinaesthetic activity for the whole class, then progress to the auditory and finally the visual activity over several lessons.

The kinaesthetic learners will need:
some modelling clay and modelling tools, card and felt-tipped pens.

The auditory learners will need:
a tape recorder/Dictaphone and copies of the 'My character description' sheet on page 12.

The visual learners will need:
copies of the 'My character description' sheet on page 12 and felt-tipped pens.

Plenary

Share the results from the activities.

- Ask some of the children to read their character descriptions or display them on the OHP or whiteboard for the class to see and read together. Highlight the words, sentences and phrases as evidence of writing in the same style as the author.
- Did the children continue the story in the same manner as the writer? What evidence is there of this? Share some of their descriptive language and write it on the board. Change some of the words to premier words, such as 'bad' to 'menacing'.
- Encourage the children to use a thesaurus to replace some of the words they have used with better words.
- Apart from the use of descriptive language and the conditional tense, what else is there in a text that informs the reader of a writer's style – for example, short sentences, lots of speech, questions?

Extension activity

Literacy – You may like to extend this theme by looking at other writers' styles. Choose a book you know well, such as *The Iron Man* by Ted Hughes. Invent another giant. Or for *The Lion, the Witch and the Wardrobe*, develop a new character in the same style as the author.

Bog Creature

Markham was a quiet village. In winter it was dark and gloomy and the road that led to it was always cut off by snow. In summer, you could set off over the moors and the clouds would build up and the sky would darken. A mist would hang so low you would have to use your headlights and travel very slowly.

Nobody walked on the moors and the bog. It was dangerous. If you lost your footing, you would be sucked under in a matter of seconds. Over the years, several hikers had lost their lives on the bog. When they were found, often weeks or months later, there would be a hush around the village. Several hikers had been found with two letters inscribed on their hands – BC. That was the sign of Bog Creature.

Nobody was really sure what Bog Creature looked like. Some say it was a small creature the size of a dog. Some say it was green and slimy with brown, bulbous eyes and no ears. It had a nose with a flap like a letterbox so it could hide under the oozing mud for hours like a hippo. The only sign it was there was the bubbles on top of the water. It moved slowly across the top of the bog like a snake, looking for its next prey.

Bog Creature wasn't the only creature that lived around those parts. There was another creature, far worse, far more frightening!

Kinaesthetic learning

(Physical, Visual/Spatial, Intrapersonal, Linguistic)

Make a clay model

- Tell the children that they are going to work on their own to make a model of the new character introduced at the end of the story.

- Provide modelling clay and tools for them to make their character models.

- When they have made the model, they should take a piece of card and write a short description of their character in the style of the author – for example, using descriptive language. This could be put on display with the model.

- Invite the children to show their models and share their ideas with the rest of the group.

- Ask the children to finish the story.

Auditory learning

(Linguistic, Physical, Interpersonal)

Record a radio interview

- Tell the children that they are going to imagine that they are a group of hikers speaking on radio about the other creature that lives on the moor.

- Hand out copies of the 'My character description' sheet (page 12) and ask them to work as a group to write down ideas for what the creature is called and what it looks like.

- Encourage them to write in the same style as the author, using alliteration, adjectives and similes.

- Encourage them to take it in turns to add to the description.

- Set up some recording equipment and appoint someone who will interview the character. After they have practised the radio interview, the children can tape it and play it to the rest of the class.

- Ask the children to finish the story, continuing in the same style as the author.

Visual learning

(Intrapersonal, Visual/Spatial, Linguistic)

Finish the story

- Tell the children that they are going to continue the story and write a character description for the new creature.

- Give them copies of the 'My character description' sheet (page 12) to jot down their ideas.

- When they have made sufficient notes, ask them to write their description on a clean sheet of paper. Encourage them to write in the same style as the author, using alliteration, adjectives and similes.

- Tell the children to underline the descriptive language and the conditional tenses they have used with felt-tipped pens.

- Ask the children to finish the story, continuing in the same style as the author.

My character description

Name of the new creature

_____

Description

_____

_____

_____

_____

_____

_____

_____

_____

_____

_____

THINK ABOUT...
Using adjectives, similes and alliteration.

WORD AND IDEA BANK

Use adjectives
Use similes
Use alliteration

How big is it?
size of a rabbit
size of a cat
like a hippo

What colour is it?
hideous green
revolting red

Eyes? Nose? Mouth?
pointed
round

What does its body look like?
fat
thin
long
short

How does it move?

What can it do?

Playscripts

Whole class starter

- Give each child a copy of the playscript sheet on page 15 or display it on an OHP or interactive whiteboard. Tell the children that this is a playscript.

- Tell the children that they are going to learn how to develop their writing of playscripts. Read the play 'Cut off by the tide' together. Ask some of the children to take the parts of the characters.

- Ask the children the following questions.

  - How is it different from a story?

    1) It is set out differently. It has the names of the characters down the left-hand side of the page.
    2) It has information about how the characters speak or move.
    3) Whenever a different character speaks, the writer starts a new line with that person's name highlighted in bold to show they are speaking.

  - Who are the characters in the play? How old do you think they are?

  - At the beginning of the play, there is some writing in brackets. What is it about? Why is it included?

- Tell the children that there are more brackets in the playscript. Challenge them to find them and underline or circle them. What are the brackets for? (They tell us how the character is moving, or how the character is speaking.) How do the brackets help the actors?

- This play is about an accident. What do you think happens next? What other accidents can happen at the seaside?

- Think about other possible places for accidents, such as a roof, railway, canal or tree. Discuss with the children what accidents can happen in those places.

- Tell the children that they are going to finish the playscript by deciding what happens next in the story.

Literacy objective
- To create playscripts applying conventions.

What you need
- Photocopies of pages 15 and 17
- Children's cartoon magazines
- Card
- Lolly sticks
- Felt-tipped pens
- Sticky tape
- Scissors
- Long sheets of paper

Extension activity

Literacy – Encourage the children to look at some playscripts that you have in school. Does the writer use brackets? Ask them to improve the playscript by including better stage directions for gestures and delivery of lines.

Independent/group work

From the activities on page 16 either:

* select the most appropriate activity for each child/group according to whether they are kinaesthetic, auditory or visual learners and organise three separate working groups

or

* begin with the kinaesthetic activity for the whole class, then progress to the auditory and finally the visual activity over several lessons.

* Tell the children that they are now going to work on their own playscripts.

The kinaesthetic learners will need:
children's cartoon magazines, card, lolly sticks, felt-tipped pens, sticky tape and scissors.

The auditory learners will need:
copies of the 'My playscript' sheet on page 17.

The visual learners will need:
copies of the 'My playscript' sheet on page 17 and long sheets of paper.

Plenary

Show the results from each activity.

* Which ending did the children prefer? Why?
* How different did they find it from writing a 'normal' story?
* What words did they put in brackets?
* How did the words in brackets help the actors?
* What have they learned about playscripts and how to improve them?

Cut off by the tide

(Kevin's gang have gone to the beach without their parents. Kevin wants to show the gang a cave he's found. They are dressed in their summer clothes; shorts, t-shirts and sunglasses. They run across the beach, chasing each other, laughing and joking.)

KEVIN: *(confidently)* Follow me to the cliffs. I've got something brilliant to show you.

SALLY: *(nervously, pointing out to sea)* But what about the tide? It's coming in soon. We could get cut off.

KEVIN: *(looking at the others for support)* Don't be silly. We've got ages yet.

(The others nod and run off ahead. Sally lags behind. Eventually Kevin stops; the others stop, too.)

KEVIN: *(confidently)* Here we are! The best cave you'll ever see. Come in.

(Kevin disappears inside. The other children peep their heads nervously inside the cave. Sally gets down on her hands and knees and hunts around in the sand.)

TOM: *(turning to look at Sally)* Are you coming?

SALLY: *(showing him some shells)* No. I'll stay here' there are some lovely shells.

(The gang disappear inside the cave.)

(Sally looks at her watch and shakes her head. Water is beginning to lap around her feet. She shakes the water out of her trainers. Then she goes to the mouth of the cave and calls to the gang.)

SALLY: You'd better be quick. The tide's coming in!!

Kinaesthetic learning

(Interpersonal, Physical, Linguistic)

Use puppets
- Tell the children that they are going to use the playscript to perform a puppet show using card puppets.

- Tell them that, if they wish, they can use cartoon characters instead of the children in the story! Ask them to decide what might happen next.

- Give the children magazines featuring cartoon characters, card, lolly sticks, felt-tipped pens, sticky tape and scissors. Ask them to draw the characters onto card, cut them out and attach them to the lolly sticks.

- After they have practised the play, invite the children to perform it for the rest of the class.

- With their help, scribe the play the children have created using the playscript conventions.

Auditory learning

(Interpersonal, Linguistic, Physical)

Act it out
- Tell the children that they are going to work together to decide what happens next in the play.

- Hand out copies of the 'My playscript' sheet on page 17 for the children to write down their ideas.

- Encourage them to share ideas and agree on what happens next. Help them to allocate roles. Let them perform their play.

- With their help, scribe the play the children have created using the playscript conventions.

Visual learning

(Intrapersonal, Linguistic, Visual/Spatial)

Make a concertina book
- Tell the children that they are going to work on their own to make a concertina playscript to continue the story.

- Hand out copies of the 'My playscript' sheet on page 17 for the children to write down their ideas.

- Show the children how to make a concertina book from a long sheet of paper. Ask them to do a simple drawing of what happens on each page. At the bottom of each page, ask them to write the words of one character with the playscript conventions. For example, page 1 –

TOM: (*shouting out*) She's right, Kevin. We'd better hurry. Kevin, where are you?

SALLY (*worried*) He can't hear us. Where is he, I wonder?

My playscript

Title _____

Names	What they say/do

WORD BANK

Characters
boys
girls
parents
police
ambulance crew
fire-fighters

Places
beach
cliffs
hospital
police station

Stage directions
shouting
laughing
crying
angrily
happily
sadly
nervously
running as fast as
he can
holding hands

THINK ABOUT...
The use of brackets and
what you will write in
them to help the actors
play their parts.

Recounts

Whole class starter

Literacy objective

- To write recounts for a close friend.

What you need

- Photocopies of pages 20 and 22
- Objects that are special to individual children
- Newspapers

- Give each child a copy the 'Sports Day' sheet on page 20 or display it on an OHP or interactive whiteboard.

- Tell the children that they are going to do some work on recounts. Ask them if they can recall what a recount is. Encourage them to give you some examples, such as 'The school holiday', 'When I had a tooth out at the dentist's' and 'My birthday party'. Read the 'Sports Day' recount with the children. Tell them that the boy who wrote this recount wrote it in a letter to a close friend.

- Ask the children the following questions.

    - What is the recount about?

    - What happened to Liam Parker? Why was it funny?

    - What happened to Liz's mum?

    - Why might the newspaper headline be 'Dog gets first place!'?

    - How would the recount have been different if it had been written for an adult or someone important?

    - This recount is informal. What does that mean? Why is it informal?

    - When would a recount have to be formal?

- Look at some newspapers. They contain recounts. How are these recounts different from a recount written for a friend? For example, would a newspaper recount say 'In assembly, Mr Crowther put us into teams...'? Share the differences between the two types and write them on the board.

- Tell the children they are now going to work in groups to write their own recount as if writing it for a close friend.

Independent/group work

From the activities on page 21 either:

- select the most appropriate activity for each child/group according to whether they are kinaesthetic, auditory or visual learners and organise three separate working groups

or

- begin with the kinaesthetic activity for the whole class, then progress to the auditory and finally the visual activity over several lessons.

The kinaesthetic learners will need:
objects that are special to individual children (see notes on page 21) and copies of the 'Recount for a friend' sheet on page 22.

The auditory learners will need:
copies of the 'Recount for a friend' sheet on page 22.

The visual learners will need:
copies of the 'Recount for a friend' sheet on page 22.

Plenary

Share the results from the activities.

- Ask a few of the children to read their recounts or copy them onto an OHP and read them with them. What did they enjoy about listening to them?
- Ask the children how it would be different if the recount was for a teacher or a news report.
- Identify some of the words/phrases that would have to be changed if the recount was for a more formal audience.

Extension activity

Literacy – Collect some newspapers that contain news reports involving children. Invite the children to choose one they are interested in and then ask them to write a report as if the incident had happened to them. They should imagine that they are telling a friend what happened (and therefore use informal language).

Sports Day

'Sports day was great this year. In assembly, Mr Crowther put us into teams named after rivers. I was in Mersey and I was the captain, too. After lunch we all went out onto the field. The parents had been invited and they were sitting on chairs in the sun eating ice lollies. It wasn't fair – we couldn't have any.

At first, it was like any other sports day – lots of running races, skipping races and a sack race. I came second in the obstacle course. Sam Benson won, but he had a head start. I'm pleased I didn't have to do the three-legged race; you had to do it with a girl. Liam Parker was in it – he had to do it with Jane Wilson. Everyone whistled at them. He was really mad. You should have seen him pull her along. They were just about to reach the finish line when he fell over. She fell on top of him and then all the others fell on top of them. Everybody laughed their heads off. You should have seen Liam's face. It was bright red.

The best part though was at the end when it was the parents' race. This year it was a skipping race. The dads went first and they were useless. Then the mums had their race. Everything was all right until a dog suddenly appeared on the field. It went straight after Liz's mum. She was about half way when she saw the dog. Although she tried to carry on running, it grabbed hold of the rope. It ran off to the finish line and got first place. Everyone clapped. A man from the newspaper was there. He took a photo of the dog. I think the headline will be "Dog gets first place!" It was great.'

Kinaesthetic learning

(Intrapersonal, Linguistic, Logical, Physical)

Show and tell

- Tell the children that they are going to do a 'show and tell' of a special occasion using an object such as a trophy, holiday souvenir or present they received.

- Remind them that they will need to think about what they are going to talk about before the lesson and bring whatever they need.

- Give out copies of the 'Recount for a friend' sheet on page 22 and ask them to write down key words to remind them of their special occasion, so they remember what to say.

- Invite each child to tell the rest of the group all about their special occasion.

- Help them to write out their recounts.

Auditory learning

(Interpersonal, Linguistic, Logical, Physical)

Role play

- Tell the children that they are going to work in pairs to do some role play. They are going to imagine that they are having a conversation about something exciting that has happened to one of them.

- Give them copies of the 'Recount for a friend' sheet on page 22 so that they can look at some of the ideas and then make notes about their special experience.

- In pairs, they should take it in turns to do their role play, reporting what happened and asking questions.

- When they have done this, invite some of them to show their role plays to the rest of the class.

- Help them to write out their recounts.

Visual learning

(Intrapersonal, Linguistic, Visual/Spatial, Logical)

Write a letter

- Tell the children that they are going to write a letter to either their best friend or an imaginary best friend telling them about something special that has happened.

- Ask them to think about what they are going to write about and to make notes on a copy of the 'Recount for a friend' sheet on page 22.

- Tell the children to write the letter on a sheet of paper and to make sure that the style is informal.

- Invite the children to either give their letter to a friend or read it aloud to the rest of the class.

Recount for a friend

What was the event?

Birthday, Christmas, party?

Who did it happen to?

You, friend, family?

Why was it memorable? funny, happy, silly, exciting, unusual?

Think about ....

Informal language and words
you would use when you're
with a friend...

Writing instructions

Whole class starter

- Give each child a copy of the 'Outdoor activities' sheet on page 25 or display it on an OHP or interactive whiteboard.

- Ask the children what they think instructions are for. Challenge them to think where they would see instructions, for example in a recipe book, a board-game or a craft book. Tell them that the sheet they have contains the instructions for a scavenger hunt.

- Read through the instructions for a scavenger hunt. If possible, when they have done this, let them do the scavenger hunt, following the instructions closely to see if they are accurate.

- Ask the children the following questions.

  - How are instructions laid out differently from a story? Why?

  - Why do the instructions have headings?

  - What would happen if you did not list the things you would need?

  - What would happen if you missed out one of the instructions?

  - What would happen if you put the instructions in a different order?

- Encourage the children to consider the language of instructions. Ask them whether there are lots of exciting words in the instructions, such as adjectives and similes. Why aren't there any interesting words and long complicated sentences? Most of the instructions begin with a verb. Ask the children to underline or highlight the verbs. Why do they think the instructions begin with verbs?

- Tell the children they are now going to work in groups to write some instructions and then test them out.

Literacy objective

- To write instructions and test them out.

What you need

- Photocopies of pages 25 and 27
- Indoor games including 'Bingo'
- Felt-tipped pens

Extension activity

Literacy – Ask the children to write the instructions for a young child's outdoor activity – for example, an infants' game such as 'Scarecrow tig'. When they have written the instructions, invite the children to test them out on some younger children.

Independent/group work

From the activities on page 26 either:

- select the most appropriate activity for each child/group according to whether they are kinaesthetic, auditory or visual learners and organise three separate working groups

or

- begin with the kinaesthetic activity for the whole class, then progress to the auditory and finally the visual activity over several lessons.

The kinaesthetic learners will need:
board-games such as 'Snakes and ladders' and 'Ludo' and copies of the 'Indoor games' sheet on page 27.

The auditory learners will need:
a bingo game and copies of the 'Indoor games' sheet on page 27.

The visual learners will need:
indoor games such as tiddlywinks, dominoes or cards, and felt-tipped pens.

Plenary

Share the results with the rest of the class.

- Ask the children to read out their instructions to the rest of the class.
- Choose one or two of the instructions to test out. Are they accurate? Have the children missed out any important information?
- What is one of the most important things the children need to remember when writing instructions? (To number each point/step.)
- Look at a variety of instructions. How many begin with verbs? Write the verbs on the board. Which are the most common? Could the children change them to other verbs with the same meaning, for example could 'Put' be replaced with 'Place'?
- Why should a writer not use exciting words and long sentences when writing instructions?
- Do the children ever give instructions to other children? When? What for?
- In which jobs are instructions important? (For example, school teacher, fitness instructor.)

Outdoor activities

Scavenger Hunt

Aim of the game
To find as many objects as possible from a list within a time limit.

How many people
Two or more players.

What you need
- Pieces of paper (one piece for each person).
- Pencils.
- Plastic bags.
- An outdoor area, for example a garden, a park or a school field.

What you do
1. Get a piece of paper and a pencil.
2. Ask the teacher for a list of things to find, such as a leaf, an acorn, a pebble and a feather.
3. Write the list on the piece of paper.
4. Search the area to find the objects.
5. When the time has run out, count to see how many things you have found.
6. The child with the most objects is the winner.

Alphabet Hunt
This is a similar game to play. This time, write the alphabet down the left-hand side of the paper. Then search the area to find things beginning with each letter – apple, branch, carrot and so on.

Kinaesthetic learning
(Interpersonal, Physical, Linguistic)

Play the game according to the instructions
- Tell the children they are going to work together in a group to provide instructions for a board-game, such as 'Snakes and ladders'. They will need to play the game first.

- Ask one of them to use the 'Indoor games' sheet on page 27 to write down how they played the game.

- Afterwards ask one of them to read the notes aloud in the order they were written and ask the others to play the game following the spoken instructions exactly to see whether the instructions are correct.

- Do the instructions work? If not the children should rewrite them.

Auditory learning
(Interpersonal, Linguistic, Physical)

Give a 'Bingo' demonstration
- Tell this group that they are going to imagine that they run a bingo hall and that they are going to explain to the players how the game is played.

- Give them a bingo set and ask them to discuss how the game is played.

- Ask one of them to make notes on the 'Indoor games' sheet on page 27.

- One of them should then read out the notes and they should all suggest improvements.

- Ask the group to role play a bingo game to the rest of the class, starting with the caller saying 'Good afternoon everyone. Welcome to Bingo Kingdom.' They should give the class instructions on how to play. Everyone should agree whether the instructions are correct.

Visual learning
(Intrapersonal, Visual/Spatial, Linguistic)

Write the rules of a game
- Tell the children that they are going to work on their own to write the instructions for an indoor game, such as tiddlywinks, dominoes or cards.

- Provide them with paper and felt-tipped pens.

- Tell them to write clear instructions with coloured headings.

- When they have produced their set of instructions, ask them to give them to another group for testing.

- The tester group should follow the instructions closely. Do they work? What amendments need to be made?

BINGO

3		31		63
7			55	68
	18	47		

Indoor games

Title

_____

Aim of the game

_____

_____

How many people

_____

What you need

_____

_____

_____

THINK ABOUT...
- All the information the reader will need.
- Begin each instruction with a verb.

How to play

1 _____

_____

2 _____

_____

3 _____

_____

4 _____

_____

Writing legends

Literacy objective

- To write own versions of a myth or a legend.

What you need

- Photocopies of pages 30 and 32
- Large sheets of paper
- Coloured paper
- Felt-tipped pens
- Scissors and glue
- A variety of objects for use in a legend play (for example, a ring, goblet, flute and shield)
- An OHP, OHTs and OHT pens

Whole class starter

- Give each child a copy of the 'Stylus and the silver sandals' sheet on page 30 or display it on an OHP or interactive whiteboard.

- Tell the children that they are going to work on legends. Do they know what a legend is? Write their ideas on the board but do not tell them whether they are correct until they have read the story 'Stylus and the silver sandals'.

- Read the story with the children. Tell them that this is a legend.

- Ask the children the following questions.
  - What is the story called?
  - Where is it set?
  - Is it a modern story or an old story? How do you know?
  - Who is the hero? What does he have to do?
  - What problems does he have?
  - What helps the hero?

- Check with the list below to see if this story is a legend. Find evidence.
  - It takes place in the olden days.
  - The story has monsters.
  - The story has strong heroes.
  - There are battles or fights.
  - Good wins over evil.

- Tell the children that they are now going to create their own legends.

Independent/group work

From the activities on page 31 either:

- select the most appropriate activity for each child/group according to whether they are kinaesthetic, auditory or visual learners and organise three separate working groups

or

- begin with the kinaesthetic activity for the whole class, then progress to the auditory and finally the visual activity over several lessons.

The kinaesthetic learners will need:
a large sheet of paper, coloured paper, felt-tipped pens, scissors and glue.

The auditory learners will need:
a variety of objects for a legend (for example, a ring, goblet, flute and shield) and copies of the 'My legend' sheet on page 32.

The visual learner will need:
copies of the 'My legend' sheet on page 32, A3 paper and felt-tipped pens.

Plenary

Share the results from the activities.

- What adventures did Stylus have?
- What kinds of monster did the hero meet?
- What magic did the hero have to help him?
- What happened to the villains in the stories?
- What have they learned about writing legends?

Extension activity

Literacy – Watch a film about a legend, such as 'Jason and the Argonauts', 'Jason and the Golden Fleece' or 'Hercules'. Ask the children to list all the monsters in the legend and to draw them. Create a class scrapbook with the title 'Monsters in Legends'. The children could make another scrapbook with the title 'Magic in Legends' and draw pictures of all the magical things that help the hero.

Stylus and the silver sandals

Stylus lived with his mother and father on a small island in northern Greece. They lived on a large farm with lots of fields and animals. One winter, his mother and father were killed in a storm by a falling tree while Stylus lay sleeping in his cot. Stylus's wicked uncle took over the farm and Stylus was sent away to live with his old grandfather in a tiny shack near Mount Olympus.

Stylus learned how to hunt and fish. He became a strong young man. However, he never knew anything about his parents until his grandfather became ill.

'Unless you get me the bottle of everlasting life I will die,' said his grandfather.

'Where can I find it?' asked Stylus.

'Your wicked uncle has the last bottle: he stole it from your father,' he replied.

'I must get it for you,' said Stylus, with a determined look in his eyes.

'But you are not strong enough,' said his grandfather. 'You will need help.'

Stylus's grandfather opened an old leather suitcase and took out a pair of silver sandals and a silver ring.

'If you need help, use these,' he said quietly.

Stylus arrived at his uncle's farm. It was guarded by two three-headed dogs with large fangs.

'How will I get past them?' Stylus asked himself.

Then he remembered the sandals and put them on. Immediately he flew over the garden wall and up to the front door. The dogs barked and snarled at him but they could not reach him. Stylus kicked open the door and went inside. His uncle was sitting by the fire guarded by a poisonous snake with one eye. Stylus pointed the ring at the one-eyed snake and it began to shrivel and die. Then he took out his sword and demanded the bottle. His uncle was a coward and handed over the bottle right away.

Stylus flew home to his grandfather and gave him the medicine. This was the first of his many adventures.

Kinaesthetic learning
(Interpersonal, Physical, Visual/Spatial

Make a picture story of a legend

- Tell the children that they are going to work together to create another adventure for Stylus and to make a gigantic picture with the title 'Stylus's adventures'.

- Ask them to think about other creatures or people whom Stylus might meet. What other objects might be given to help him?

- Give them a large sheet of white paper, coloured paper, felt-tipped pens, scissors and glue. Allocate various parts of the picture to different children – it should be made up of the hero (to be stuck in the centre of the picture) and magical objects, monsters and villains (to surround the central picture and to be joined to it with arrows).

- Ask the children to draw their pictures on coloured paper, then cut them out, stick them on the large sheet of paper in an appropriate place and label them.

- Scribe the children's legend with them.

Auditory learning
(Physical, Interpersonal, Linguistic)

Create a play about a legend

- Tell the children that they are going to work together to perform a sound story legend.

- Provide a variety of objects that they could use – a ring, a goblet, a flute, a shield and a helmet. Tell the children that they MUST use some of these objects in their play.

- Encourage the children to choose a new character for the legend and discuss how the objects will fit into the story.

- Ask them to write down their ideas on the 'My legend' sheet on page 32. For example, the flute could send people to sleep.

- Help the children to choose characters for the play, allocate roles, practise their performance, give the play a title. Invite them to perform it.

- Write out the children's play with their help.

Visual learning
(Visual/Spatial, Linguistic, Intrapersonal)

Create a comic strip of a legend

- Tell the children that they are going to work on their own to make a comic strip of their own legend, with speech bubbles, about a monster their character meets.

- Encourage them to create their own monster using ideas from the stories they have heard and videos they have watched. They can use the 'My legend' sheet on page 32 to help them.

- Show them how to divide an A3 sheet of paper into eight sections. Tell them to write one part of their story in each section by drawing a simple picture and speech bubbles. For example, 'Oh no! It's Triheader, the three-headed monster with a tail like a long whip and teeth as sharp as glass.'

My legend

Title

_____

What the hero has to do

_____

_____

Information about the villain

_____

_____

Information about the monsters

_____

_____

What magic the hero has to help him

_____

_____

_____

IDEA BANK

Hero has to find
golden goblet
silver mask
magic tree
golden apples

Magic to help him
flute
jewellery box
ring
goblet
horn
sword
helmet
winged horse

Monsters
lion's body
snake for a tail
man with a hawk's head

Minotaur
Hydra
Centaur
Medusa

THINK ABOUT...
Features of legends.

• take place in olden days
• monsters   • heroes
• battles
• good wins over evil

Writing extended poems

Whole class starter

- Give each child a copy of the 'On my birthday' sheet on page 35 or display it on an OHP or interactive whiteboard.

- Tell the children that they are going to look at poems that they can extend. What does 'extend' mean? Encourage them to share their ideas but do not come to any agreement yet. Explain that they may have some more ideas about this word after reading the poem together.

- Read the 'On my birthday' poem from page 35 with the children. Tell them that this is a rhyming poem.

- Ask the children the following questions about the poem.

    - What is the title of the poem?

    - What is it about?

    - How many verses are there?

    - How many lines are in each verse?

    - Can you find the rhymes? What is the pattern for the rhymes?

    - The poem has words that are repeated in each verse. What are the words?

    - Many children's poems have repetitive lines. Why do you think that is?

    - If the poem was to have another verse, what would the pattern be?

- Tell the children that they are now going to work on their own extended poems.

Literacy objective
- To write an extended poem.

What you need
- Photocopies of pages 35 and 37
- A word-processing program and a printer

Extension activity

Literacy – Give the children a selection of poetry books or a variety of poems that you have photocopied or typed out. Ask them to identify the poems that have repetitive words in their verses and to highlight the repetitive words. Then challenge them to write extensions for these poems.

Independent/group work

From the activities on page 36 either:

- select the most appropriate activity for each child/group according to whether they are kinaesthetic, auditory or visual learners and organise three separate working groups

or

- begin with the kinaesthetic activity for the whole class, then progress to the auditory and finally the visual activity over several lessons.

The kinaesthetic learners will need:
cards with people's names on them, such as Mike, cousin Jane or brother Jack and copies of the 'My poem' sheet on page 37.

The auditory learners will need:
copies of the 'My poem' sheet on page 37.

The visual learners will need:
copies of the 'My poem' sheet on page 37, a computer and a printer.

Plenary

Share the results from the activities.

- Many repetitive poems are for young children. Why do the children think that is?
- Did the children find it easy to write extensions for the poems? Why, or why not?
- Were they able to think of enough rhymes? Explain how rhyming dictionaries can be used to help with such a task.
- Is this kind of poem easy to remember? Why?
- Is the rhythm important for helping us say the poem and remember it?

On my birthday

On my birthday
Said the boy
I'd like a new football
And a motorised toy.

On my birthday
Said the girl
I'd like a CD
And a doll with a curl.

On my birthday
Said Grandad Mick
I'd like a new pipe
And a walking stick.

On my birthday
Said cousin Nathan
I'd like some Lego
And a new play station.

On my birthday
Said Auntie Tess
I'd like some perfume
And a pink silky dress.

Kinaesthetic learning

(Interpersonal, Linguistic, Physical)

Missing words
- Tell the children that they are going to work in a group to extend the 'My birthday' poem on page 35.

- Seat the children in a circle. Place the name cards face down on the floor in the middle of the circle.

- As a group, say together 'On my birthday, said ...' Then ask someone to pick up and read out a name on one of the cards.

- The children should suggest a 'present' that rhymes with that name, such as 'Paul – ball; Mike – bike; Jane – chain; and Ken – pen'. If that child cannot think of a present they say 'Pass' and the next person has a go.

- The children could work together to record some of their verses on the 'My poem' sheet on page 37.

Auditory learning

(Interpersonal, Linguistic, Musical)

Say aloud
- Tell the children that they are going to work in a small group to extend the poem called 'What's for tea?' on the 'My poem' sheet on page 37.

- Encourage them to discuss possible additional verses and write them on the sheet.

- Invite the group to perform their poem to the rest of the class. They could use percussion instruments to help them with the beat.

Visual learning

(Intrapersonal, Linguistic, Visual/Spatial)

Computer poem
- Tell the children that they are going to work on their own to extend the poem called 'Fancy dress party' on the 'My poem' sheet (page 37).

- Ask the children to note their ideas on the sheet, then write the poem out on the computer, including graphics if they are able.

- Ask the children to print out their poems and to staple their verses together to make one poem.

- Invite one child to make a front cover for the 'book' on the computer.

My poem

Title

_____

New verses

_____

_____

_____

_____

_____

_____

_____

_____

_____

_____

_____

_____

_____

_____

IDEAS

What's for tea?

What's for tea?
Chinese is nice,
Noodles, chow mein
And plenty of rice.

Ideas for new verses

Indian in a hurry – curry
English is good – pud
French never fails – snails
Italian is tasty – pastry

_____

Fancy dress party

A fancy dress party
Come as a ghost
A long white sheet
To scare the host.

Ideas for new verses

football star – far
clown – gown
king – anything
cat – that

THINK ABOUT...
• The rhyming pattern.
• The beat to make it flow.

Non-chronological reports

Literacy objective

- To write a non-chronological report.

What you need

- Photocopies of pages 40 and 42
- Clipboards
- Old pictures, photos, newspapers and postcards of your town
- Scissors and glue
- Large sheets of paper
- Dictaphones
- Paper and pencils
- Extra adult helpers to supervise the children on a walk around town

Whole class starter

- Ask the children to tell you what kinds of things they could look at that might tell them about the history of their town. They might think of the following: the ages or types of buildings; evidence of the past, such as disused buildings, bridges or railways; places of worship; and other features such as monuments. Discuss how certain features, such as a market square, village pond or special monument, tell us about the history of a place.

- Give each child a copy of the 'History around you' sheet on page 40 or display it on an OHP or interactive whiteboard.

- Tell the children that they are going to look at non-chronological reports. What do they think a non-chronological report is? Encourage them to share their ideas but do not come to any agreement yet. Explain that they may have some more ideas about non-chronological reports after sharing the text.

- Read the 'History around you' sheet together. Tell the children that this is a non-chronological report. Agree that a report tells us about something. Explain that a non-chronological report is one that can be written in any order. Ask them what information this report gives us.

- Ask the children to look at how the report is set out. How is it different from a story? (It has an introduction, subheadings and lots of factual information.)

- Read the introduction. Ask the children what an introduction is. How is it different from the other paragraphs?

- Ask the children to count how many subheadings there are and to tell you what they are. How do subheadings help the reader? What would happen if they were switched around?

- Tell the children that they are going to write their own non-chronological reports.

Independent/group work

From the activities on page 41 either:

- select the most appropriate activity for each child/group according to whether they are kinaesthetic, auditory or visual learners and organise three separate working groups

or

- begin with the kinaesthetic activity for the whole class, then progress to the auditory and finally the visual activity over several lessons.

The kinaesthetic learners will need:
copies of the 'My non-chronological report' sheet on page 42, clipboards, old photos, pictures, newspapers and postcards of the town, scissors, glue and large sheets of paper.

The auditory learners will need:
dictaphones.

The visual learners will need:
clipboards, pencils and paper, and copies of the 'My non-chronological report' sheet on page 42.

Note: Make sure the children are adequately supervised. Check with your LEA guidelines before arranging the walk.

Plenary

Share the results from each activity.

- How did the activities help the children understand non-chronological reports?
- Why was it important to think about headings?
- Did the children experiment with changing headings around? What difference did it make?
- Why are introductions important when writing reports?
- What have the children learned about the history of where they live?

Extension activity

History – Investigate the history of your own town further. The children could go to the library and find out more by looking at books about their town, old newspapers or old videos. Ask them to collect information and make a scrapbook about the history of their town.

History around you

History is all around you. Some people never see it because they do not really use their eyes. You will need to be a detective to find some of the historical things in the town where you live.

Fords

A long time ago, travellers crossed rivers using the shallow part called a ford. Large stepping-stones were sometimes placed across a ford so that travellers did not get wet. Place names tell you that they mark the spot where a river could be crossed – for example, Bedford, Watford and Stratford.

Bridges

No one knows who made the first bridge. In Devon there are some old ones made from stone slabs that rest on rocks in the stream. They are called clapper bridges. Most bridges are made from stone, brick, iron or concrete.

Stiles

The word 'stile' means step or ladder. Stiles make it easier for people to cross walls, fences and hedges. Stiles can be made from wood, iron or stone. In the olden days, footpaths and stiles were used more than roads. There are different kinds of stiles – ladder stile, turnstile, stone steps and slab stile.

Milestones

Milestones were first set up in England in Roman times. The word 'mile' comes from the Latin word 'mille' – meaning a thousand. You can still find old milestones along many main roads. Many milestones give the distance to London.

Kinaesthetic learning

(Physical, Interpersonal, Linguistic, Visual/Spatial)

Make an historical collage

- Tell the children that they are going to work together in small groups to make a collage showing the history of their town.

- Organise a walk through the town. Give the children copies of the 'My non-chronological report' sheet (page 42) to use on clipboards to jot down what they see. Agree the four headings for their observations, such as 'houses', 'places of worship', 'other buildings' and 'other historical features'.

- They should also collect as many old pictures, photos, newspapers, and postcards of the town as possible.

- When they come back to school, they should use the information they have gathered, plus the items they have collected, to make a large visual group non-chronological report.

Auditory learning

(Linguistic, Physical, Interpersonal, Logical)

Give an historical talk

- Tell the children that they are going to work in pairs or small groups to go on a walk around their town and record a commentary on its history.

- Organise a walk through the town. Give the children dictaphones and ask them to record the things they see that relate to the history of the town or place where they live.

- When they come back to school, ask them to organise what they have seen into a report to tell the rest of the class. Remind them to use a subheading for each new item.

Visual learning

(Intrapersonal, Linguistic, Visual/Spatial, Logical

Make an historical poster

- Tell the children that they are going to work on their own to design a poster encouraging people to visit the town because of its history.

- Organise a walk through the town. Provide clipboards, pencils and paper, and copies of the 'My non-chronological report' sheet (page 42). Ask them to sketch what they see – for example, old buildings.

- They could use a digital camera and print out the photographs when they are back at school.

- When they come back to school, ask them to design a large poster promoting the town and its history. The poster should include pictures, text and headings.

My non-chronological report

_____

_____

_____

_____

THINK ABOUT...

- How many headings will you have?
- What will your headings be?
- What will you write about each one?

LOOK AT THESE
- old buildings • old shops
- churches • inns/pubs
- schools • bridges/fords
- signposts/market crosses/milestones

Making evaluations

Whole class starter

- Give each child a copy of the fable and evaluation sheet on page 45 (it may be more appropriate to enlarge it to A3 size so that it looks more like a wallchart) or display it on an OHP or interactive whiteboard.

- Tell the children that they are going to write an evaluation. Do they know what an evaluation is? Write down their ideas on the board, but do not tell them.

- Read the fable with them and then read the evaluation below it.

- Ask the children the following questions.

  - What was the story about?

  - Who wrote it?

  - What kind of story is it?

  - Who wrote the evaluation of the story?

  - What do you think an evaluation is now?

  - Why is the evaluation split into different parts?

  - What does each heading mean?

  - Do you think the evaluation is fair? Why, or why not?

  - Is there anything else you noticed about the piece of writing?

  - What targets would you set Gary to improve his work?

- Tell the children that they are now going to work on their own evaluations.

Literacy objective
- To evaluate work.

What you need
- Photocopies of pages 45, 47 and 48
- Card
- Whiteboard
- Sticky tack
- Work to evaluate (either on paper or OHT)

Extension activity

Cross-curricular – Ask the children to evaluate pieces of work from across the curriculum. Discuss whether they can use the same headings or whether they need to have different headings. Why is that? Ask the children to come up with their own chart for marking work across the curriculum – for example, science or history. Share their ideas.

Independent/group work

From the activities on page 46 either:

- select the most appropriate activity for each child/group according to whether they are kinaesthetic, auditory or visual learners and organise three separate working groups

or

- begin with the kinaesthetic activity for the whole class, then progress to the auditory and finally the visual activity over several lessons.

The kinaesthetic learners will need:
copies of the evaluation sheet on page 47 and the help sheet on page 48, card, a whiteboard, sticky tack and work to evaluate.

The auditory learners will need:
copies of the evaluation sheet on page 47 and work to evaluate (on paper or OHT).

The visual learners will need:
copies of the evaluation sheet on page 47.

Plenary

- Talk about the work the children have evaluated. Is it difficult evaluating work? Why?
- What do the children have to remember when evaluating someone's work?
- What headings did the children use? What are the most common words for each category?
- Display one of the children's evaluations. What is the ratio of positive comments to negative comments? What do they think the ratio should be?
- What targets did the children set? Did they find it difficult to think of some? Why is target setting important?
- Ask the children to evaluate other children's work on a more regular basis using the template.

A fable by Gary Murphy

Horse lived alone in a large field where the grass was green and fresh and there was plenty of shade from the old oak tree.

One day the farmer arrived at the gate with a horse box.

'What are you doing?' asked Horse, galloping over to the farmer.

'I've brought you a friend,' said the farmer.

'But I don't need a friend,' said Horse. 'I'm quite happy by myself.'

The farmer opened the horse box and let out the horse. She was a beautiful dapple-grey with a long mane. Horse didn't like her.

'Hello,' said Dapple Grey.

Horse ignored her and walked away. Dapple Grey followed Horse around the field trying to make friends.

'I don't need you. I don't need friends,' said Horse. 'GO AWAY.'

Horse kicked up his back legs angrily and caught Dapple Grey. She winced and limped off to the far corner of the field.

One night, a horse box arrived. Horse went over nosily to see what was going on. Suddenly the door opened and two men jumped out. Quietly they bundled him into the van.

Dapple Grey was too far away to help. She turned her head and sighed. 'If only he'd listened,' she said.

Moral: 'Everyone needs friends.'

Evaluation by Jack Parker

Purpose and organisation – Gary has answered the question and produced a fable for another child. It has a moral at the end.

Style/Grammar – Gary is fluent. However, he could improve his writing by using complex sentences with commas. He uses tenses consistently, i.e. the past tense. He could have used more exciting words.

Punctuation – He has used capital letters and full stops. He has also used speech marks. He could have used exclamation marks too (for example, after 'GO AWAY').

Spelling – The spelling is excellent and there are no mistakes.

Handwriting – Gary's writing is joined up and clear.

Target – To use more adventurous vocabulary and complex sentences.

Kinaesthetic learning
(Physical, Visual/Spatial, Linguistic)

Use word cards for evaluation
- Tell the children that they are going to evaluate a piece of work using word cards.

- Photocopy the 'Evaluations – Words sheet' onto card and cut out the words. Give the children a large whiteboard, some sticky tack and a piece of work to evaluate.

- Ask them to write the headings for the evaluation on the whiteboard (as listed on the 'My evaluation' sheet on page 47). Ask them, as a group, to choose from the word cards those words that best describe the piece of work. For example, under the heading 'Handwriting' they might wish to use the words 'clear' and 'legible'.

- Ask the children to make copies of the work and the evaluation to show the rest of the class. Invite the class to suggest changes to some of the words that were chosen.

Auditory learning
(Interpersonal, Linguistic, Physical)

Discuss and agree an evaluation
- Give the children a piece of work on an OHT or photocopied sheet. Tell them that they are going to have a group discussion about this piece of work.

- Give the children copies of the 'My evaluation' sheet on page 47 to help them consider areas for evaluation. Ask them to choose one heading each (for example, spelling) and think of three positive points and one negative point.

- Encourage them to discuss their ideas together and improve what they have to say.

- After their discussion, invite the children to report back to the rest of the class, taking it in turns to talk about an aspect of the evaluation.

Visual learning
(Intrapersonal, Linguistic, Visual/Spatial)

Make a written evaluation
- Tell the children that they are going to imagine that they are an examiner and write an evaluation of a child's piece of work.

- Give them a piece of writing from another child to evaluate and a copy of the 'My evaluation' sheet on page 47 to help them.

- Ask them to write a clear, concise report in their best handwriting. They should then give the report to the child and explain their reasons.

My evaluation

Purpose and organisation

- Did it answer the question?
- Was the writing organised properly?
- Was the non-fiction layout correct?
- Did the story have a beginning, a middle and an end?

Style and grammar

Was the style appropriate for the reader?
Did it use:
- a variety of sentences, i.e. short, long (complex)?
- a variety of connectives?
- adverbs?
- descriptive language – for example, adjectives?
- consistent tenses – for example, the past?

Punctuation

- Capital letters/full stops
- Commas
- Exclamation marks/question marks
- Speech marks

Spelling

Handwriting

Evaluations – Word sheet

makes sense	fluent
disjointed	logical
complex sentences	simple sentences
inconsistent tenses	consistent tenses
capital letters	full stops
speech marks	punctuation
excellent	thorough
no mistakes	errors
legible handwriting	illegible handwriting
limited vocabulary	adventurous vocabulary
clear	exciting
disorganised	answered the question

Writing in the style of another writer

Whole class starter

- Give each child a copy of the story on page 51 or display it on an OHP or interactive whiteboard.

- Tell the children that they are going to learn how to write in the style of another person. Ask if any of them know what that means. Write their ideas on the board.

- Read the story with the children and ask them the following questions.
  - What is the setting for the story?
  - Where in the world could it be?
  - Who are the main characters?
  - What do we know about the characters? What evidence is there?
  - What do we know about the place where they live?
  - Why were the characters worried that morning?
  - What do you think happens next? (For example, men appear to cut down the jungle; there is a forest fire; there are hunters.)

- Say to the children that it is quite easy to continue a story, but a lot more difficult to continue it in the style of the author.

- Discuss what they think distinguishes the style of this author. Refer to the points below.
  - He is a traditional writer; there is no slang or modern words.
  - He uses descriptive language – for example, adjectives and similes ('coloured parrots like flashing rainbows').
  - He uses direct speech.
  - He uses simple sentences.
  - He writes in the past tense.

- If the children were going to continue the story, how would they continue the style? Share their suggestions.

- Tell the children that they are now going to continue the story themselves.

Literacy objective
- To write in the style of the author.

What you need
- Photocopies of pages 51 and 53
- Paint and brushes
- Frieze paper
- A dictaphone or tape recorder
- Musical instruments
- Drawing materials

Extension activity

Literacy – Photocopy an excerpt from a book the children have not seen. Ask them to continue the story in the style of the author. Repeat this activity with a range of different genres, such as science fiction, horror, magic, humour and adventure.

Independent/group work

From the activities on page 52 either:

- select the most appropriate activity for each child/group according to whether they are kinaesthetic, auditory or visual learners and organise three separate working groups

or

- begin with the kinaesthetic activity for the whole class, then progress to the auditory and finally the visual activity over several lessons.

The kinaesthetic learners will need:
paint, brushes, a roll of frieze paper and copies of the 'My story' sheet on page 53.

The auditory learners will need:
a dictaphone or tape recorder, some musical instruments and copies of the 'My story' sheet on page 53.

The visual learners will need:
copies of the 'My story' sheet on page 53 at A4 and A3 size and drawing materials.

Plenary

Share the results from the activities.

- What alternatives did the children come up with for the next part of the story?
- How did they continue in the style of the writer (for example, ask them to give examples of the descriptive language they used)?
- How difficult did they find it to continue in the same style?
- How do they think looking at other people's writing styles would help them with their own writing?

The end of the forest

Timo had woken early. He had gone hunting with his father in the forest. They often got up early to hunt for breakfast. Timo had sharpened his knife the day before, like his father, and he was ready.

He loved the forest. He had lived there all his life. Life was peaceful; the people were happy. They shared what little they had and it was enough. They had comfortable wooden huts to live in. The women cooked and looked after the children. The men hunted and made spears. The children played games. There was no interference from the outside world. They had heard about the outside world but, as yet, the outside world had not come to them and they were grateful.

Timo liked the forest first thing in the morning. He liked to tread quietly over the forest floor watching and listening as he went. He liked the colourful flowers and the shiny green leaves just like someone had polished them. He liked to hear the sound of raindrops dripping off the trees and collecting in small pools on the forest floor. He liked to see the brightly coloured parrots like flashing rainbows as they flew through the trees and to hear the call of the birds and the monkeys. He liked to watch the dark eyes in the undergrowth watching him as he watched them. He was never afraid for he knew the forest well.

This morning was different. The forest was quiet. His father noticed the quiet, too.

'What is it, Father?' asked Timo.

'I'm not sure,' said his father worriedly. 'It's too quiet, far too quiet.'

Cautiously, they crept further into the jungle, watching carefully as they went.

Suddenly the forest awoke. The sound was deafening. Birds and animals all called frantically to one another. Then the trees came alive. Birds and animals darted through the undergrowth. Above them and below them was a sense of panic. Then they were gone. Only Timo and his father remained.

'What is it?' called Timo, his knees trembling.

His father pointed ahead of them. 'They've come!' he shouted, his voice echoing around the forest. 'They've come!'

Kinaesthetic learning

(Interpersonal, Physical, Linguistic, Logical)

Make a mural

- Tell the children that they are going to work in a group to paint what happens next in the story. (The idea is to show the events in order from left to right like the Bayeux tapestry.)

- Give them paint, brushes and a roll of frieze paper to set out across several tables.

- Ask them to discuss what they think happens next and write it down on the 'My story' planning sheet (page 53).

- Each child should then choose part of the story sequence to paint, for example a wall of fire, the animals and birds in panic or the people's escape. Underneath their drawing, they should write a descriptive sentence about what they have seen, such as 'The wall of fire surrounded them.'

Auditory learning

(Interpersonal, Linguistic, Physical)

Create a story with sound effects

- Tell the children that they are going to tape the next part of the story using sound effects.

- Give them a dictaphone or tape recorder, and some musical instruments.

- Ask the children to write down their ideas on the 'My story' sheet (page 53). For example, they could write 'A bulldozer appears; men get out and begin to chop down trees.' Encourage them to think of appropriate language to keep the story in the style of the author, for example 'A bulldozer with monster's eyes chopped down trees like paper.'

- Organise a way for some of the children to do the sound effects while others read the story and others play different characters in the story.

Visual learning

(Intrapersonal, Linguistic, Visual/Spatial)

Make a storyboard

- Tell the children that they are going to work on their own to make a storyboard to show what happens next in the story.

- Give them copies of the 'My story' sheet (page 53) to use to plan their ideas.

- For their finished pieces of work, enlarge the 'My story' sheet to A3 and ask the children to draw four pictures to show what happens next and to write a sentence underneath in the style of the author.

Name _____

My story

1

2

3

4

IDEAS BANK

FIRE	HUNTERS	CHOP DOWN FOREST
raging	armed with guns	machines
sizzling	bullets	headlights like eyes
terrifying	panic	trample down

Points of view

Literacy objective

- To write from another character's point of view.

What you need

- Photocopies of pages 56, 58 and 59
- Card
- Dressing-up clothes

Whole class starter

- Give each child a copy of the 'What really happened?' sheet on page 56 or display it on an OHP or interactive whiteboard.

- Tell the children that they are going to work on another character's point of view. Read the text 'What really happened?' Tell the children that the excerpt at the top is from a newspaper and the excerpts below are what two of the witnesses said happened.

- Ask the children the following questions.

    - What is a newsflash?

    - Where would you see/hear/read a newsflash?

    - What is the newsflash about?

  In the two text extracts:

    - Who has given their point of view about what happened?

    - Do you think they are telling the truth? Why, or why not?

    - Who else could give a point of view about what really happened?

- Tell the children that they are now going to work on points of view.

Independent/group work

From the activities on page 57 either:

- select the most appropriate activity for each child/group according to whether they are kinaesthetic, auditory or visual learners and organise three separate working groups

or

- begin with the kinaesthetic activity for the whole class, then progress to the auditory and finally the visual activity over several lessons.

The kinaesthetic learners will need:
dressing-up clothes and copies of the 'Points of view' sheet on page 58.

The auditory learners will need:
copies of the 'Points of view' sheet on page 58 and copies of page 59.

The visual learners will need:
copies of the 'Points of view' sheet on page 58.

Plenary

Share the results from the activities.

- How important is it to be clear in what you say or write when expressing an opinion?
- When you are acting out a point of view, how else can you persuade someone other than by what you say?
- Would the children prefer to persuade someone by writing what happened or by saying it?
- Where may something like this actually happen? (A law court.)
- What is evidence? Why is evidence important?

Extension activity

Literacy – Bring some newspapers or magazines to school. Ask the children to find some stories from the papers and magazines that have a point of view. Ask them to cut out one of the stories that interests them, stick it on a piece of paper and underneath it write the report from another character's point of view.

Ask the children to consider a book they are reading in class (one that is written in the third person – for example, *James and the Giant Peach, Harry Potter, Sheep Pig, The Silver Sword*). Tell them to select an exciting episode from the book and to imagine they are one of the characters. How do they feel?

What really happened?

NEWS FLASH – Monkey escape

A monkey escaped from Animania Circus last night. Somehow it managed to leave the Big Top and hasn't been seen since. The management blame the escape on a door that had been left open by one of the audience. Anyone sighting the monkey should telephone 01754 843919.

What the Ring Master said:

'It was the opening night. There was a full house and everything was running smoothly. The clowns were wonderful, the acrobat stunts were magnificent and the horse riders were fast and furious. Then it was time for the performing monkeys. We'd been practising with a couple of new monkeys and suddenly one of them jumped off its stand and ran down the main aisle. Someone had left the tent door open and that was it – the monkey escaped.'

What a member of the audience said:

'I was sitting in the back row with my family when suddenly the man next to me stood up and held up a large banana. The young monkey saw it and jumped off his stand and ran towards us. The man left his seat and ran outside. The monkey, of course, followed him. That was the last we saw of them both!'

Kinaesthetic learning

(Intrapersonal, Linguistic, Physical)

Tell your point of view to the judge

- Tell the children that they are going to imagine that they are in a court of law because they are a witness to the incident at the circus. You should take the role of the judge.

- Write the character names on cards, for example 'monkey trainer', 'photographer', 'member of the audience', 'WWF representative' and 'RSPCA representative'. The children choose a character card. Provide dressing-up clothes to help them get into role.

- Give the children some time to make notes about what happened on the 'Points of view' sheet (page 58). Make clear that they should not disclose their account to anyone else. Then ask them to give evidence to the judge and the rest of the class, acting in character as well as making their statement. Invite the class to decide who is telling the truth.

Auditory learning

(Interpersonal, Linguistic, Physical)

Read, make notes and discuss

- Tell the children that they are going to work in pairs to read the story 'Fire!' (page 59) and then discuss who they think is to blame and why.

- Hand out copies of the story and the 'Points of view' sheet (page 58) for the children to write down their thoughts.

- At the end of the session, invite the children to share their thoughts with the other children and give their reasons.

Visual learning

(Intrapersonal, Linguistic, Visual/Spatial)

Write it down

- Tell the children that they are going to work on their own to imagine that a window has been broken at school by a ball.

- Ask them to write what happened from at least two people's points of view, for example from the perspective of a teacher, a child or the caretaker.

- Give out copies of the 'Points of view' sheet (page 58) for the children to make notes.

Points of view

THINK ABOUT...
- Where the character was
- What happened
- Witnesses
- Evidence
- Suspects

Reasons/Evidence

_____

_____

_____

_____

_____

_____

_____

_____

_____

_____

_____

_____

_____

_____

_____

Who did It?

Name of character

_____

Innocent or guilty

_____

by
U. R. Right

FIRE!

NEWS BULLETIN

St Paul's wooden scout hut was burned to the ground last night. Fire-fighters battled all night to save the hut, but most of the damage had been done before the fire engine arrived. Anyone with information about the fire should telephone 01752 485392.

What the scout leader Miss Brown, aged 69, said:

'We'd just had a scout meeting. Jack and Harry Jones were the last ones to leave. I checked all the rooms and locked the windows and doors and walked home. I'd only been home about twenty minutes when the emergency services rang. I'm so upset. The hut was my pride and joy.'

What Harry said:

'The meeting had finished and all the boys had gone. Jack and I usually tidy up for Miss Brown, the scout leader, but she told us that she'd do it. We walked off down the drive. I remember turning round and seeing a light in the building; it could have been a flame. We didn't turn back because our dad had come to pick us up.'

What local resident Joe Barley, aged 79, said:

'I live next door to the scout hut. That night the kids had been playing outside. They were really noisy as usual. They woke my wife up again; she has really bad migraines. Eventually the boys went home. Miss Brown was the last to go. It was strange really because I saw her running down the drive and usually she walks really slowly.'

Writing a journal

Literacy objective

- To begin writing a reading journal.

What you need

- Photocopies of pages 62 and 64
- Large sheet of coloured paper
- White paper speech bubbles
- Glue and scissors
- Coloured pens
- Exercise books

Whole class starter

- Give each child a copy of the 'Reading journal' sheet on page 62 or display it on an OHP or interactive whiteboard.

- Tell the children that they are going to look at reading journals. Ask them if they know what a reading journal is. Encourage them to share their ideas and write them on the board, but do not tell them yet. Read the sheet with them. Say that this is a reading journal.

- Ask the children the following questions.
  - Does this text agree with our ideas on what a reading journal is?
  - Who has written the journal?
  - Which book is the journal about?
  - Can you find these things and underline them?
    - information about the story
    - predictions
    - questions
    - reflections.
  - What use is a reading journal?
  - Who is the reader?

Independent/group work

From the activities on page 63 either:

- select the most appropriate activity for each child/group according to whether they are kinaesthetic, auditory or visual learners and organise three separate working groups

or

- begin with the kinaesthetic activity for the whole class, then progress to the auditory and finally the visual activity over several lessons.

The kinaesthetic learners will need:
a large sheet of coloured paper, white paper speech bubbles, coloured pens, glue, scissors and copies of the 'My reading journal' sheet on page 64.

The auditory learners will need:
copies of the 'My reading journal' sheet on page 64.

The visual learners will need:
exercise books and copies of the 'My reading journal' sheet on page 64.

Plenary

Share the results from the activities.

- How did it help having areas to discuss rather than talking about the book generally?
- How will the reading journal be useful?
- Who will read the journal?
- What other headings could be used?

Extension activity

Literacy – Show the children the beginning of a film. Ask them to quickly jot down their feelings, reflections, questions and predictions. Then show the rest of the film to the children. Were they correct?

Reading journal

READING JOURNAL belonging to Kerry Davies

Matilda

Chapter 1: The Reader of Books

Today I started reading Matilda by Roald Dahl. I chose this book because I've read most of his books and enjoyed them.

The story is about a girl called Matilda who's really clever. When she is four she goes to the library to get some books because her dad won't buy her any. She runs out of books to read. (I couldn't even read when I was four years old!)

Roald Dahl has included some horrible adults in the book. (He does this in most of his books and that's what I think makes his books brilliant.) By the end of the first chapter I felt really sorry for Matilda. It isn't fair that she is treated the way she is. I would have run away. I wonder what will happen next? I wonder whether she will get her own back on her parents for being so unkind?

Chapter 2: Mr Wormwood the Great Car Dealer

There's a description of Mr Wormwood in this chapter. He's just what I expected. He's really mean to Matilda and calls her 'stupid' and lots of other names. He's a really bad person. I hope something horrible happens to him soon.

There are some excellent drawings in the book. They're done by Quentin Blake. He draws the pictures for all Roald Dahl's books.

Kinaesthetic learning

(Intrapersonal, Linguistic, Physical)

Write in speech bubbles

- Tell the children that they are going to work in a small group to record ideas for a journal.

- Give them a large piece of coloured paper, some small pieces of white paper in the shape of speech bubbles and some coloured pens. Each speech bubble will be a heading (see the sheet on page 64 for ideas).

- Read the first chapter of a book and then invite each child to choose an area on which to focus, for example 'predictions'. Ask them to write down their thoughts in coloured pen in the speech bubbles, for example 'I think that...' They should stick the bubbles on the large sheet.

- Encourage the children to add more ideas for each heading when they read the next chapters of the book.

Auditory learning

(Interpersonal, Logical, Physical)

Circle time

- Tell the children that they are going to be involved in a circle time to discuss ideas for a reading journal.

- Read the first chapter of a new book aloud and then encourage the children to discuss the headings included in a journal (see the 'My reading journal' sheet on page 64).

- Go round the circle and ask each child to contribute an idea, for example a question they could ask from what they have read.

- Appoint one child to scribe the ideas on a whiteboard to share with the rest of the class.

Visual learning

(Intrapersonal, Linguistic, Visual/Spatial)

Produce a journal

- Tell the children that they are going to work on their own to produce a reading journal.

- Give them an exercise book and show them how to start writing their own journal using the headings provided on the 'My reading journal' sheet on page 64.

- The children should record ideas for each chapter on a new page.

Name _____

My reading journal

Book _____

REFLECTIONS

FEELINGS

PREDICTIONS

IDEAS BANK
- What will the character do next?
- I predict that there will be…
- I enjoyed the…
- I felt…

QUESTIONS

Using persuasive language

Whole class starter

- Give each child a copy of the leaflet on page 67 or display it on an OHP or interactive whiteboard.

- Tell the children that they are going to work on points of view. They should know what a point of view is from previous work. Tell them that they are going to look at a leaflet. Read the leaflet together.

- Ask the children the following questions.

    – What is a leaflet?

    – What is this leaflet about?

    – What reasons are given for saving the theatre?

    – What reasons could you give for closing the theatre?

    – What structures does the writer use to inform us that this is a point of view?

    – What words does the writer use to move the argument on? ('Firstly', 'Secondly' and so on.)

    – What persuasive devices does the writer use? (Questions and exaggeration.)

- Talk about where the children might have seen other leaflets expressing points of view – through the letterbox, inside newspapers or on notice boards, for example. What were these leaflets about? Did they use persuasive language?

- Tell the children that they are now going to work on a leaflet to express a point of view.

Literacy objective

- To write a commentary on an issue on paper – for example, as a leaflet – setting out and justifying a point of view using persuasive language.

What you need

- Photocopies of pages 67 and 69

- Pictures of buildings from travel agents, newspapers, magazines

- Scissors and glue

- Large sheets of paper

- A desktop publishing program with clip art and printer

Independent/group work

From the activities on page 68 either:

- select the most appropriate activity for each child/group according to whether they are kinaesthetic, auditory or visual learners and organise three separate working groups

or

- begin with the kinaesthetic activity for the whole class, then progress to the auditory and finally the visual activity over several lessons.

The kinaesthetic learners will need:

pictures of buildings from travel agents, newspapers and magazines, scissors, glue and large sheets of paper.

The auditory learners will need:

copies of the 'My leaflet' sheet on page 69.

The visual learners will need:

access to a desktop publishing program and printer, and copies of the 'My leaflet' sheet on page 69.

Plenary

Share the results from the activities.

- Write on the board some examples of persuasive devices. Which do the children think would be the most successful? Why?
- Is it easier to express a point of view on paper or verbally? Ask the children their opinions.
- In which professions would you need to be able to use persuasive devices? (Sales, politics or advertising.)

Theatre close down

Say NO!

Yellow Brick Theatre
Probably the best theatre in the country!

WHY should we save the theatre?

1 FIRSTLY, it was opened to celebrate Queen Victoria's jubilee and is therefore a part of the town's history. The theatre was also visited by the Queen Mother in 2000 as part of the millennium celebrations.

2 SECONDLY, it has entertained children and adults for over 150 years! Thousands of people have walked through the doors.

3 THIRDLY, it is the only theatre in the town. If it closes down, people will have to travel to other towns.

4 FOURTHLY, it has provided employment for people who will now be out of work, especially the disabled staff who will have difficulty finding other employment.

5 FINALLY, it is a place where young actors have begun their careers. Some have gone on to perform in West End musicals and a few have appeared on screen. Without the theatre, no other budding actors will get this chance.

Should we let this happen?
NO! NO! NO!
Save the theatre by signing the petition.
Do it now before it's too late!

Friends of Yellow Brick Theatre

Kinaesthetic learning

(Intrapersonal, Linguistic, Logical, Visual/Spatial)

Design a leaflet

- Tell the children that they are going to design a leaflet about saving a building, such as a church, museum or hotel.

- Give them some pictures of buildings from travel agents, magazines or newspapers. Ask them to each choose one of the buildings and stick it in the centre of a large sheet of paper.

- Around the outside of the picture, ask them to write the reasons for keeping the building.

- Finally, ask the children to give their leaflet a title.

Auditory learning

(Interpersonal, Linguistic, Logical)

Make a television broadcast

- Tell the children that they are going to act out 'Theatre Close Down' for a TV broadcast.

- Tell them to imagine that they are 'for' closing the theatre down. They will need to discuss reasons for closing the theatre and write down their ideas on the 'My leaflet' sheet (page 69).

- When they have thought of enough ideas, ask them to act them out for the rest of the class.

Each child could take the part of a different character – for example, land developer, councillor, resident, architect or shopkeeper. They should say who they are and why the theatre should be shut down.

- Invite the class to decide who has the best argument and vote.

- The group could then prepare a leaflet together.

Visual learning

(Intrapersonal, Linguistic, Visual/Spatial, Logical)

Create a poster on the computer

- Tell the children that they are going to work in pairs to produce a leaflet to save a school.

- Arrange for them to have access to a desktop publishing program that has clip art, and a printer.

- Ask them to use the 'My leaflet' sheet (page 69) to note down reasons why they want to save the school.

- When they have completed their notes, ask the children to produce the leaflet on the computer, using clip art to illustrate it.

My leaflet

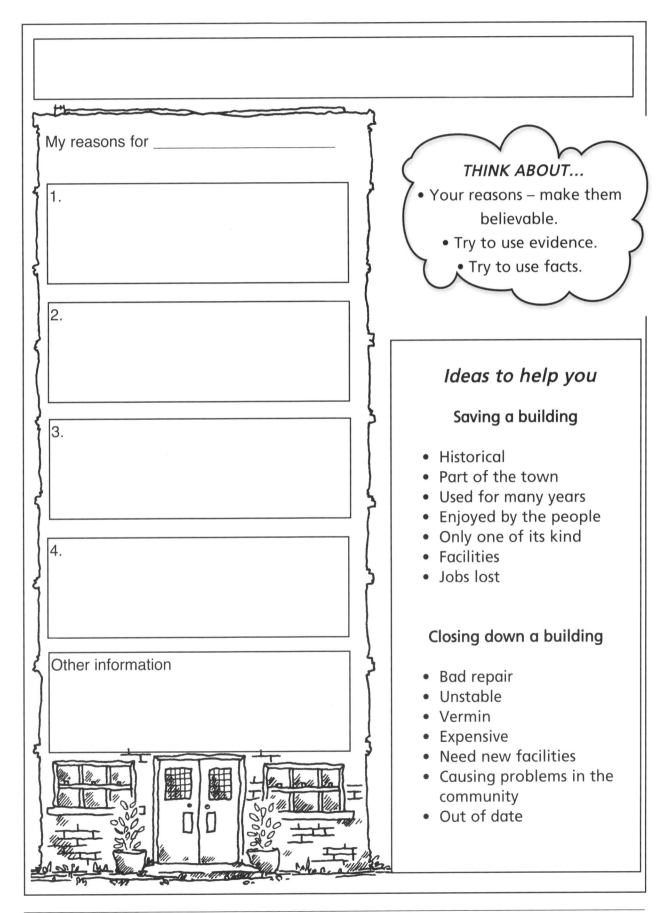

My reasons for _____

1.

2.

3.

4.

Other information

THINK ABOUT...
- Your reasons – make them believable.
- Try to use evidence.
- Try to use facts.

Ideas to help you

Saving a building

- Historical
- Part of the town
- Used for many years
- Enjoyed by the people
- Only one of its kind
- Facilities
- Jobs lost

Closing down a building

- Bad repair
- Unstable
- Vermin
- Expensive
- Need new facilities
- Causing problems in the community
- Out of date

NOTES

NOTES

NOTES